God@Work

Practicing Spirituality in Your Workplace

Gregory F. Augustine Pierce

RENEW
INTERNATIONAL

Finding God at Work

The Scripture quotations contained herein are from the New Revised Standard Version Bible (containing the Old and New Testaments with the Apocryphal/Deuterocanonical Books), copyright © 1989 by the Division of Christian Education of the National Council of Churches of Christ in the U.S.A., and are used by permission. All rights reserved.

English translation of the *Catechism of the Catholic Church* for the United States of America copyright © 1994, United States Catholic Conference, Inc.—Libreria Editrice Vaticana. English translation of the *Catechism of the Catholic Church*: *Modifications from the Editio Typica* copyright © 1997, United States Catholic Conference, Inc.—Libreria Editrice Vaticana. Used with permission.

NIHIL OBSTAT
Reverend Lawrence E. Frizzell, D.Phil.
Archdiocese of Newark Theological Commission
Censor Librorum

IMPRIMATUR
Most Reverend John J. Myers, D.D., J.C.D.
Archbishop of Newark

All rights reserved. No part of this book may be reproduced, stored in a retrieval system, or transmitted without the written permission of RENEW International.

Copyright © 2004 by RENEW International
ISBN 1-930978-19-7
Cover design by James F. Brisson
Cover photo by Susan Capurso
Book design by John T. Lynch
Interior illustrations are taken from the first two volumes of SPECIAL TOUCH for Your Creative Needs, published by The Communications Office, Sisters of St. Joseph of Carondelet, 11999 Chalon Road, Los Angeles, California 90049

To order, call 888-433-3221
www.renewintl.org

RENEW International
1232 George Street
Plainfield, NJ 07062-1717

Contents

Preface iii

IMPACT Series v

Process Overview vii

Session 1 1
Spirituality of Work:
An Oxymoron?

Session 2 9
Work: A Burden to be Borne or
A Share in God's Creative Power?

Session 3 17
Dealing with Others at Work

Session 4 25
Balancing Work, Personal,
Family, Church, and
Community Responsibilities

Session 5 33
Deciding Right and
Wrong at Work

Session 6 41
Working to Make
the System Work

Music Resources 50

Further Reading on the Spirituality of Work 50

Titles in IMPACT Series 51

About RENEW International 53

Preface

"God is everywhere." This is the answer we usually give to the question, "Where is God?" Whether we truly believe this statement or not, however, is quite another thing.

It's easy to find God in "sacred" places. Those places often include church and home and nature, especially when they include large doses of silence, solitude, and simplicity. But it is often much more difficult to become aware of God's presence in the midst of the hustle and bustle—the noise, crowds, and complexity—of our daily work.

Finding God@Work is an attempt to raise our awareness, as contained in a popular saying, that "Bidden or not bidden, God is present." While it may be easier to discover God on a mountaintop or in a monastery, it is just as possible—albeit more of a challenge—to do so at our workplace.

This six-session small group faith-sharing book has been developed to help you think differently about your work and to share your experiences with others. Based on the social inquiry method, it attempts to make the spirituality of work a transformative reality in our world.

Many of the ideas in these sessions are treated at greater length in my book *Spirituality@Work: 10 Ways to Balance Your Life On-the-Job*, and appropriate chapters of that book are suggested for reading in preparation for these sessions. In addition, I maintain an e-mail group of over 1000 people who conduct an ongoing dialogue on how to practice the spirituality of work. Upon completion of your sharing program, you are invited to join "Faith and Work in Cyberspace" by sending me an e-mail at SpiritualityWork@aol.com. There is no charge for this service, and no one else ever sees your e-mail address.

Thank you for your participation in this process. God's blessings on all your good work.

Note

All suggested songs are taken from the album *Anthology*, Vol. II by Marty Haugen, GIA Publications (see Music Resources for further information). Other appropriate music may be substituted if desired.

Gregory F. Augustine Pierce is the president and co-publisher of ACTA Publications (Assisting Christians To Act), a publisher of books and tapes for the Catholic/Christian market. Pierce is also a popular speaker and writer on Catholic spirituality of work. He is the author of *Spirituality@Work: 10 Ways to Balance Your Life On-the-Job* (Loyola Press, 2001), which received two book awards from the Catholic Press Association.

Pierce is married to Kathy, a Catholic junior high school teacher. The couple are the parents of three teenagers, twins—Abigail and Nathaniel—born on their father's 40th birthday and Zachary. The family is a member of St. Mary of the Woods Catholic parish on Chicago's northwest side.

IMPACT Series

No person in the history of the world has made more impact upon humanity than Jesus Christ. Through his Spirit, he calls us to discipleship and asks us to become a people of witness and service in the world. Jesus came that we "may have life, and have it abundantly" (John 10:10). This full life calls forth a whole new respect for the dignity of each person and for harmonious relationships between and among men, women, children, and all of creation. This "reign of God" proclaimed by Jesus is not only relegated to the hereafter, but is also here and now.

We are called to live this reign of God in our everyday lives. The gifts of faith, hope, and love are not restricted to Sunday Mass or special times of prayer. They are intended to permeate our entire week and be reflected in all our activity. Since the full expression of the Holy Spirit's presence may conflict with the customs and mores of our society, we often compartmentalize our faith. As a result, it can become insipid and lack real impact in our daily lives.

The Second Vatican Council projected a more holistic view: "The work of Christ's redemption concerns essentially the salvation of men and women; it takes in also, however, the renewal of the whole temporal order. The mission of the church, consequently, is not only to bring people the message and grace of Christ but to permeate and improve the whole range of temporal things" (Vatican Council II: *Decree on the Apostolate of Lay People*, 5).

The IMPACT Series aims to do precisely this. In connecting us to a wide range of human concerns and issues, we hope that participants will be led to prayerful reflection and fruitful sharing. Growth through action is another basic principle in the IMPACT Series. Discussion and even good sharing are not enough. The intention of this series is to lead participants to concrete and specific actions that influence human attitudes and behaviors. Some of the IMPACT Series materials that deal with social issues will use the Observe, Judge, Act methodology because of its proven ability to lead to thoughtful and effective action.

For small Christian communities to be worthy of their name, carrying out the mission Christ gave to his Church must always be their primary focus. Faith sharing that turns in on the self-interest of the group will, in time, have the effect of atrophy on the group. The Holy Spirit should be a fire vigorously moving a healthy community to a ministry of loving service.

Many issues are somewhat difficult to face and to grasp. Experience shows that they are seldom addressed without a certain amount of challenge, guidance, and assistance. The IMPACT Series is designed to meet this need and, in doing so, to help small Christian communities realize better their great potential for participation in God's reign on our earth.

Process Overview

The following information gives background information on the social inquiry approach: Observe, Judge, Act, as well as suggestions for the small community leaders to prepare them for their leadership role.

Observe, Judge, Act

The social inquiry approach was adopted by Cardinal Joseph Cardijn, a Belgian priest who founded the Young Christian Workers (YCW). The YCW sought to enable young workers to re-Christianize their own lives, their working and social environments, and individuals with whom they worked.

The movement took root in the United States along with the accompanying forms of the Young Christian Students (YCS) and the Christian Family Movement (CFM). The latter sought to restore families to Christ and to create small Christian communities that would transform parishes and the wider society.

Many people are struggling to make Christian values a more meaningful part of their lives. The social inquiry cycle used in this series will enable people to go back to their environment better prepared to bear a Christian influence.

Briefing

The social inquiry approach works best when there is a pastoral person, a facilitator, or a coordinator of small communities who meets with small community leaders before each meeting for a briefing. At these meetings, leaders can dialogue about pastoral considerations for their communities, evaluate previous meetings, become better prepared in understanding the materials they will be using, and discuss any areas of concern they may have.

Suggestions for the Leader or Facilitator

You have the opportunity of aiding the small community to grow in a deeper awareness of God's dynamic presence in each member's life. Your own deep personal relationship with Jesus, through prayer and the sacraments and living faith in your daily life, will help as you attempt to facilitate group members in richer prayer, sharing, learning, and transformative action.

Preparation

Make a personal phone call to each member of the community in order to welcome him or her. Introduce yourself. Provide a way for each member to have a copy of this book at least a week before the first meeting. Invite the members to read the Preface as well as the designated Scripture readings, reflections, and the "Observe" for the first session. At the end of each session, invite participants to prepare for the upcoming week by again reading the designated Scriptures, reflections, and the "Observe" and be prepared to share briefly what his or her observations are.

Prior to the meeting time, prayerfully reflect upon the session. Preview the prayer suggestions. Prepare whatever is needed for prayer—music, words, equipment— or share this responsibility with another member of the group. On the day of the meeting, arrange the room for prayer and sharing.

It would be most helpful if some or all members of the group had a Bible at the meeting.

Because this book follows the social inquiry approach,

ideally a group will meet every two or three weeks. This will allow members of the community sufficient time to implement their outreach actions and time for observations to be made in preparation for the upcoming meeting.

Sessions

There are six sessions in this book. Some groups that are new may want to meet seven times, using the first session to become acquainted with each other, to read the introductory materials, and to come to some common agreements (see below). Each session includes the following parts:

Aim

Read the aim as a way of calling to mind the focus of the session.

Introductions and Common Agreements

If the group has not met before or if participants do not know each other, it is important to have time for introductions and an opportunity to get acquainted. People share most easily when they feel comfortable and accepted in a group. Agree on some ground rules regarding the meeting times, places, and ways of being together.

- Will each session begin and end according to the schedule decided upon by the group?
- Will you create a relaxed atmosphere?
- Will you be respectful and supportive of each member?
- Will you keep all personal sharing confidential?
- Will you serve simple refreshments at the end of the session?

Opening Prayer
Each session begins with a time of prayer. Prayer must always be at the heart of gatherings of Christians. As leader, you need to decide how the opening prayer is conducted.

Action Response
After the first week, the leader asks participants to share briefly how they did with their action response from the previous session. These reports are to be kept factual and brief. They serve to encourage the group members and enable them to sense progress. It is important that group members choose an action that flows from prayer, sharing, and their life experiences. Each session offers some ideas for an action response. However, these are merely suggestions.

Observe
The "Observe" portion of the meeting is designed to uncover facts. Rather than having discussion revolve around the personal opinions of the small community members, the "Observe" helps to focus participants on the reality of the situation.

Members are asked to gather information about other people's attitudes, perceptions, and behaviors regarding the topic at hand. For example, if the topic is the effect of our work on others, we could ask several people what effect our presence or work has upon them. Likewise, in talking to two or three others, we would discover what effect the work of someone close to them has on them. The "Observe" aspect trains people to see more clearly what is going on around them.

Participants prepare their observations for each session

before coming to the meeting. In the meeting itself, the leader invites participants to report these observations briefly and to the point, without embellishment. The discussion and judgments that follow will then be based on common perceptions (and not just hearsay or personal opinions).

Judge or Reflection and Sharing
The "Judge" aspect becomes the crux of the meeting. It includes a time for reflection and sharing. It is concerned with understanding the appropriate attitudes, values, and approaches to be taken regarding the reflective observations that have been made.

The process of judgment or reflection and sharing is, above all, based on gospel wisdom as proclaimed in the Scriptures or through the teachings of the Church. Members may do some studying that will help them more clearly understand their faith, moral issues, and/or social and global issues.

As the collective wisdom of the group is shared, consensus emerges from its sharing. This wisdom obviously involves the wisdom of the Spirit, alive in the community members. A very practical turn is taken in the process of reflection and sharing. Theory alone will not enable people to bring about change effectively in a given situation. Down-to-earth considerations, such as how to approach a person and what to say, must be taken into account. Again, the collective wisdom of the group usually avoids ill-advised efforts and results in practical and effective direction.

The "Judge" portion causes us to reflect upon the questions: "What would a committed Christian think or do?" and "How is this reflected in the teachings of the Church, Scripture, and the faith life of the people?" If done well, it usually provides a natural lead-in to action.

The leader may include questions such as the following in the "Judge" aspect of the meeting:

What can we do about the situation or attitudes?

How can we go about changing attitudes and behaviors?

In what way can our own actions reflect the teaching of the Church? of Scripture?

Act/Respond

The sharing at each meeting leads to very specific actions to be taken. These may be individual actions or ones taken by the group as a whole. The size of the action is not a prime concern. It is important that the responses are practical, concrete, specific, and within reasonable expectation of accomplishment. The leader ought to encourage every member to choose an individual action or the group as a whole to choose a common action.

Successful responses can be as simple as a conversation in the coming week that will raise a particular topic with the hope of influencing an attitude. The action can also be a very significant action representing the united commitment of the entire small Christian community. This is the particular value of staying with one topic of social concern for several weeks. When members take sufficient time for research and analyze a particular social issue, it is more likely the small community will be committed to a long-term action.

Look Ahead to the "Observe" for the Next Meeting
The leader invites participants to read the "Observe" for the next meeting and makes any necessary clarifications. At times, various participants will take responsibility for different aspects of the "Observe."

Closing Prayer
The leader may use the suggested closing prayer or substitute another. When shared prayer is suggested, remember that praying spontaneously might be a new experience for some. Members should have the freedom to pray aloud or remain silent. Be comfortable with short periods of silence.

Suggested Flow of the Sharing Sessions (1½ Hours)

Introductions (when the group is new or when someone joins the group)

5 min.	Opening Prayer
5 min.	Action Response
15 min.	Sharing the "Observes"
5 min.	Reflection 1
15 min.	Sharing
5 min.	Reflection 2
25 min.	Sharing
10 min.	Act/Respond
5 min.	Closing Prayer

SESSION 1

SPIRITUALITY OF WORK: AN OXYMORON?

Aim

This session questions our assumptions about the nature of both spirituality and daily work, with the goal of defining or describing the spirituality of work. It also looks at our work as the primary way that we participate in helping to build the kingdom of God.

> The spirituality of work is a disciplined attempt to align ourselves and our environment with God and to incarnate God's spirit in the world through all the effort (paid and unpaid) we exert to make the world a better place, a little closer to the way God would have things.

Opening Prayer

Loving God and Father, we offer you this day our accomplishments and our hopes and dreams for the future. Continue to bless us as together we explore how to find you in the work we do in our careers, in our homes, and in our leisure time. We ask this in the name of Jesus, your Son and our brother, and in the Holy Spirit. Amen

Song: "Bring Forth the Kingdom"

Scripture: Genesis 1:26—2:3, The culmination of creation and a time of rest

Take a few moments to savor a word, a phrase, a question, or a feeling that rises up in you. Reflect on this quietly or share it aloud.

Observe
(To be prepared before the meeting.)
Ask two or three people—co-workers, family, neighbors, parishioners—the following questions:

What comes to mind when you hear the word "spirituality"? (Record their responses.)

How would you describe your work? (Listen to them talk about their work. Record their responses.)

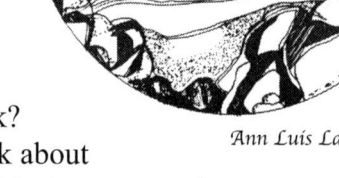

Ann Luis Lardizabal, CSJ

Later, reflect on the question: Did you hear any connections between persons' definitions of "spirituality" and their descriptions of their work?

Judge
Reflection 1
When people think about spirituality, they usually think about getting away from the hustle and bustle of daily life—at least for a while. Their thoughts turn to a church or monastery, a mountaintop or sunset—any place where they might find a few moments of "silence, solitude, and simplicity" in which to get in touch with God.

Work, on the other hand, is sometimes viewed as the opposite of spirituality. The workplace is often described as a "rat race," a "daily grind," the scene of "cutthroat" competition, a pursuit of the "almighty dollar," a place of stress, tension, disloyalty, even oppression.

So the phrase "the spirituality of work" seems to be an oxymoron—two words that do not seem to fit together in a way that makes sense. To unravel this oxymoron, we must look at both words, "spirituality" and "work," and reflect on the essence of each of them.

Spirituality is often equated with contemplative practices: prayer, meditation, fasting, spiritual reading, etc. But these are only means to an end, and that end is the raising of our awareness of the presence of God. So if we are able to raise our awareness of the divine presence in other ways, could not these ways also be considered spiritual? As Brother Lawrence of the Resurrection (1611-1691), a Carmelite monk who worked in the monastery kitchen, wrote in his classic little book, *The Practice of the Presence of God*, "In my kitchen's noise and clatter, while several people are all calling for different things, I possess God just as peacefully as if I were on my knees at the altar, ready to take communion."

Work, for many people, is the opposite of spirituality. If spirituality is "getting away from the world," then work is getting deeply "into the world. "If work is so great, then why do they have to pay us to do it?" wrote *Chicago Tribune* columnist Mike Royko. And Abraham Lincoln once admitted: "I never did like to work, and I don't deny it. I'd rather read, tell stories, crack jokes, talk, laugh—anything but work." Even our Judeo-Christian tradition is ambivalent about work. While God worked for six days creating the world (and therefore work is good), Adam and Eve were banished from the Garden of Eden to work "by the sweat of their brow" (see Genesis 3:16-19).

So when we use the phrase "the spirituality of work," people are naturally skeptical. "What exactly are you talking about?" they ask. The answer is that the spirituality of work is a disciplined attempt to raise our awareness that God is present in every workplace and to use that awareness to change how we do our own work. The difference is that rather than looking for God in a church or on a mountaintop or at a sunset, we use the reality of our work as the "grist" for our spiritual mills.

Is such a spirituality possible? Yes it is, and many people are practicing it right now. These sessions will be an attempt to "observe, judge, and act" on the spirituality of work.

Sharing
- What word, phrase, or image from the Scripture reading or the reflection touched my heart or spoke to my life?
- When did I experience the presence of God by getting away from the hustle and bustle of my daily life? What was the setting? How did I feel? How did that encounter change me?
- When did I experience the presence of God in the midst of my work on a job, with my family, or in a volunteer community or church activity? How was the experience the same as the first encounter? How was it different?

- Are there some workplaces where God appears absent? Explain.

Reflection 2

In the beginning of the Acts of the Apostles, Luke writes, "After his suffering he presented himself alive to them [his disciples] by many convincing proofs, appearing to them during forty days and speaking about the kingdom of God" (Acts 1:3).

Think about that for a moment. Of all the things Jesus had taught his followers during his life, the "reign" or "kingdom" of God was the one thing he wanted to be sure they did not forget after he left them.

So it is pretty clear that the main mission for the followers of Christ—including us today—is to help bring about the kingdom of God "on earth as it is in heaven," as Jesus taught us to pray. To put this in more contemporary language, we are to help make the world a little more like the way God would have things.

This is a big assignment, and we are right in asking how we are to accomplish it. The answer is as obvious as it is difficult: The primary way we help make the world a better place is through our daily work—on our jobs, with our families, and in our community and civic involvement.

"Not in my workplace," some may respond. "My work is too insignificant, my boss is too demanding, my customers are too unreasonable, my co-workers are too competitive." Others might say, "I do find my work meaningful and fulfilling, but that doesn't mean it isn't stressful, exhausting, or even ethically ambiguous."

This is where the spirituality of work comes in. Instead of viewing our workplaces as isolated from our religious or spiritual lives, we can develop disciplines or practices that can accomplish the twin goals of all spirituality: to raise our awareness of the presence of the divine Spirit and to allow that Spirit to change how we act. The development of these practices will be the goal of this series of six sessions.

Sharing

- How do I react to the idea of helping to bring about the kingdom or reign of God in my workplace? Is this something I think about on a regular basis? Why or why not?

- One moment or experience at work where my own spirituality or that of another positively affected my behavior or attitude was _____.

- If things were done in my workplace "as they are in heaven," what things would have to change? Why can't they change now? What can I do to help change them?

Act

Determine a specific action (individual or group) that flows from the content of your sharing. This should be your primary consideration. When choosing an individual action, determine what you will do and share it with the group. When choosing a group action, determine who will take responsibility for different aspects of the action. The following are secondary suggestions.

Some Suggestions
- Make a list of the different work you have done (including parenting and volunteer work). Next to each, name one way that you helped make the world a little better place through your work.
- Interview one person you know who appears to be practicing a spirituality of work. Ask that person how he or she experiences the presence of God in his or her workplace.
- Investigate ways that your parish supports and encourages the connection between faith and daily work, including through liturgies, religious education, the sacraments, support groups, and other activities.
- Read chapters 1-2 of *Spirituality@Work*.

Look Ahead
Take time to read the "Observe" for Session 2. Be prepared to share clearly and briefly your observations at the next meeting.

Closing Prayer

All   Thank you, Lord God, for the gift of life. Thank you for all of creation. You have given us a great gift. Increase our awareness of you, Lord, as we go about our daily work. Help us to see you and honor you in all the people in our workplace, for they are also your children and they are also part of your creation. We say, in the words Jesus, our brother, taught us:
Our Father….

SESSION 2

WORK: A BURDEN TO BE BORNE OR A SHARE IN GOD'S CREATIVE POWER

Aim

This session encourages us to look at the various meanings that people find in daily work, from "making a living" to "doing my duty" to "sharing in God's ongoing creation." These meanings all carry with them spiritual assumptions and insights.

Jean Iadevito, CSJ

Opening Prayer

God, you have created us in your image to do your work on earth. You created the universe for us and saw that it was good. May we find fulfillment in whatever occupation we choose and also see that it is good. Amen

Song: "Awake, O Sleeper"

Scripture: Matthew 5:13-16, You are the salt of the earth.

Take a few moments to savor a word, a phrase, a question, or a feeling that rises up in you. Reflect on this quietly or share it aloud.

Finding God at Work

Action Response
Review Actions from your last meeting.

Observe (To be prepared before the meeting.)

Approach three or four people and talk to them about their work. Ask them why they do what they do. Concisely report the different meanings people find in their work.

> My experience as a letter carrier with the U.S. Postal Service taught me that in the midst of business there can be a stillness in which God speaks and acts. So often I have had the deepest sense of God or had some revelation when I've been hard at work. My best time of prayer is when my feet are moving on my route.
>
>   Rose M. Hart
>   —letter carrier
>   Glen Dale, West Virginia

Judge
Reflection 1

Everyone who works—at a job, around the home, as a parent or caregiver, in a volunteer community organization, or in a church-sponsored ministry—must decide the meaning of that work if he or she is going to experience its spiritual nature.

If you ask people why they work, many will answer, "It's a living," or "To put bread on the table." These meanings are real and they can be noble. (Just ask someone who is involuntarily unemployed and unable to find work.) To work to provide for the material needs and well being of oneself and one's dependents is part of the task of being human. Even in the early Church, Saint Paul was quick to advise that Christians should work. "Anyone unwilling to work should not eat" (2 Thessalonians 3:10), he advised somewhat harshly (at least by today's standards). Paul went even further by offering his own work as a tentmaker as an example for others: "I could have been cared for, but I chose to work." Saint Joseph provided another example with his work as a carpenter, which provided for the needs of the Holy Family and has made him the patron saint of all workers.

We are often ambivalent about this meaning of work. On the one hand, if people are unemployed, we are quick to help them out by providing for their basic necessities, forming a support group, or even helping them find a job. If people are gainfully employed, however, we sometimes dismiss their work, precisely *because* they are paid for it. "He's just out to make a buck," we may say, or "She's only in it for the money."

In the Church, we have sometimes created two classes of workers. If someone is working for the Church or under Church auspices, this is often called "ministry" and the person is said to have a "vocation." Meanwhile, people who work in non-Church related organizations or in secular professions are said to have "a job" or, at best, to be part of the "lay apostolate." Our parishes have to be very careful that in our eagerness to encourage lay ministry in the Church, we do not communicate that those who are not so inclined or involved are, in the words of one parish newsletter, "pew potatoes."

One final point we laypeople need to reflect upon regarding "making a living" is whether we are paying our own parish and Church-related institutional employees a just wage. The fact that people are working for the Church does not absolve us from the obligation to pay them enough to support themselves and their families. This duty to pay a just wage is not removed simply because we are able to find people who are willing to work for such wages!

So you can see that question of "making a living" at work is as complex as it is real. A spirituality of work should both honor and celebrate this meaning of work.

Sharing
- What word, phrase, or image from the Scripture reading or the reflection touched my heart or spoke to my life?
- Have I ever been unemployed or in fear of losing my job, or had a loved one in that situation? How did my loved one or I feel spiritually?
- Where does the obligation to pay a just wage come from? How should a just wage be determined?

Reflection 2

Making money is not, of course, the only reason people work. Some of our best work is done for little or no pay at all—for example, parenting, coaching, work around the home, volunteer activity, political involvement, caring for ill or disabled loved ones. Retirees, part-time workers, lay ministers, and unemployed people all do significant work that receives little or no remuneration. In addition, many people in our society make much more money than they need for basic necessities, yet they still keep working.

At some point, everyone needs to ask, "What am I working *for*?"

Most people find other meaning in their work in addition to "making a living." For some, they find satisfaction in "doing a good job" or "helping people" or "creating a quality product or service" or even "just staying busy." These, too, can be important meanings of our work—ones with deep spiritual implications.

Other times, we do our work out of duty or necessity, simply because "it needs to be done" and "somebody has to do it." This purpose provides meaning to a wide variety of work, both paid and unpaid. For example, people in medicine and the helping professions, teachers, ministers of all kinds, police and firefighters, people in the military and government service, sanitation workers, and janitors find meaning in doing a job that others shy away from out of a sense of commitment to the common good. Much of the work of parenting and care giving is done—at least partly—out of a sense of duty, as is much of the work of citizenry and Church or community leadership.

Finally, more and more people are beginning to see their work (in its entirety) as their main contribution to God's ongoing creation of the universe. God continues to "bring order out of chaos," and this work is what we humans continue through our daily work. When seen in this light, our work is truly holy indeed, the "work of human hands" worthy to be offered to God as our gift at each eucharistic celebration.

The spirituality of work may be practiced in a way that helps us explore all these various meanings of work, enabling us to increase our awareness of the presence of God in our various workplaces, and changing how we do the work we now see as sacred.

Sharing
- Some different types of work that I have done over the years for which I was not paid are _____. Why did I do the work and what did I get out of it?
- What feeling of satisfaction do I derive from performing certain tasks, either on my job, with my family, or in my community or church? Where does this satisfaction come from?
- How can my work be part of God's ongoing creation? If I have a deeper appreciation that my work is part of God's ongoing creation, how will I act upon this in my daily work?

Act
Determine a specific action (individual or group) that flows from the content of your sharing. This should be your primary consideration. When choosing an individual action, determine what you will do and share it with the group. When choosing a group action, determine who will take responsibility for different aspects of the action. The following are secondary suggestions.

Some Suggestions
- Choose one task and complete it with the best quality and care of which you are capable. Do the work as you would imagine God would approach it. Reflect on the process and the results when you are finished.

- Talk with others in your community and discover how you can be more responsive to the needs of people who are poor or unemployed. Perhaps you could help organize an unemployed support group or get members of the parish to meet with people looking for work to provide ideas or job contacts.

- You may have experienced God's presence when a co-worker showed appreciation for help with a project, when you were congratulated for a job well done, or when you had a sense of personal satisfaction in knowing you have done your best. This week, tell a couple of co-workers that you appreciate them for the work they do. Be specific in your praise.

- Read chapters 3-5 of *Spirituality@Work*.

Look Ahead
Take time to read the "Observe" for Session 3. Be prepared to share clearly and briefly your observations at the next meeting.

Closing Prayer
Dear God, we thank you for your many blessings. Help us to realize that the work we do is in service to all your people. Holy Spirit, inspire in us the desire to develop a renewed purpose in our vocations as we go about our daily work. In this way we can be the salt of the earth and a light that shines before others.

(*Individual members of the group may add their prayers of petition, thanksgiving, and praise.*
Response: Hear us, O Lord.)

Close with the Lord's Prayer.

SESSION 3

DEALING WITH OTHERS AT WORK

Aim

This session raises the issue of how we deal with others at work. Is the "golden rule" a practical guide for our activity at work? How would the workplace look if we truly practiced the spirituality of work with one another?

Marion Honors, CSJ

Opening Prayer

Dear God, may my mind think no harm, may my lips speak no harm, may my hands do no harm. May the children of tomorrow bless the work I offer. Amen

(Adapted from *The Fire of Peace*, p. 69. Mary Lou Kownacki, OSB, published by Pax Christi USA, 1992)

Song: "Healer of Our Every Ill"

Scripture: Luke 10:29-37, The Good Samaritan

Take a few moments to savor a word, a phrase, a question, or a feeling that rises up in you. Reflect on this quietly or share it aloud.

Action Response

Review Actions from your last meeting.

Observe
(To be prepared before the meeting.)

Observe for one complete day how you and others are treated by people—clerks in stores, waiters in restaurants, people on the phone, supervisors and co-workers

> The gospel message is unconditional love, unconditional trust, unconditional Jesus Christ. You go out on a limb, you trust people, and no matter how many times they slap you in the face or backstab you, you turn the other cheek. Christianity is not a "this for that" calling. It has to start somewhere, and that somewhere is among those of us who decide to take a deep breath and jump off the "cliff" of uncertainty. Some of us will undoubtedly get smacked on rocks, but that's what being Christian is all about.
>   Richard P. Bohan
>   —educator, husband, and father
>   Des Plaines, Illinois

at your job, ministers at church, even members of your own family. Record your findings. On another day, be conscious of how you treat others as you go about *your* daily work. Again, record your findings. Concisely report your two sets of findings.

Judge
Reflection 1
How we treat others at work is both a reflection of our spirituality and a contributor to our spiritual development. Virtually no one works completely alone. No matter whether we work in a home, store, office, factory, farm, service or repair facility, church or medical center, courtroom or classroom, plane, train, truck or automobile, work is by its very nature a social endeavor. We all have colleagues, customers, clients, suppliers, competitors, employees, bosses, and fellow commuters. We are all dependent upon others to do our work, and they in turn are dependent upon us.

So how we deal with others in the workplace (whether that be a paid job or a volunteer activity) is important—not only to the smooth functioning of our economy, but also to our spiritual health, both as individuals and as the human race.

The first level of dealing with others at work is simple honesty and justice. We need to know that each worker is going to give "a full day's work for a full day's pay" and that employers pay a just wage and provide decent working conditions. We need to be assured that the products and services we produce and/or purchase are delivered with the best quality possible, at a reasonable price, and without harm either to ourselves, others, or our environment.

Christians and other people of good will, however, see the workplace as an opportunity to practice a much deeper level of spirituality. Rather than settling for the minimum required, such folks view the workplace as a primary venue for fulfilling Jesus' command to love our neighbor. "And who is my neighbor?" the lawyer asked Jesus. In response, Jesus told the story of a man who was on a trip (possibly even a business trip) from Jerusalem to Jericho and happened upon a man who had been beaten by robbers. Rather than worrying about how it might affect his "bottom line," the man did what needed to be done, even paying for the victim's health care (see Luke 10:29-37)!

> I try to remember to thank people who work hard for me on projects by noting their accomplishments and contributions to their managers. Depending on the length of a project and the amount of effort expended, I also take these people to lunch. I'm not always able to do this, but I keep trying.
>
> Teri Tanner
> —information technology audit manager
> Arlington, Massachusetts

It is this kind of spirituality that is so desperately needed in today's workplace. It is a spirituality that does not accept work as a rat race where, as comedienne Lily Tomlin says, "even if you win you're still a rat." It is a spirituality in which we deal with others, as we would have them deal with us.

Sharing
- What word, phrase, or image from the Scripture reading or the reflection touched my heart or spoke to my life?
- What happens when I am "honest and just" at work?
- What does it mean to "love my neighbor" in the workplace?

Reflection 2
What would a workplace look like in which we actually dealt with others as we would have them deal with us? First of all, it would be a very different workplace from that experienced by most people. The idea of competition—between those inside a company or firm or agency or institution and against those in other businesses or institutions—would not be based on one person being up because the other is down. Certainly there would still be competition based on talent, training, creativity, and hard work, but there would be much less cheating, lying, or seeking to create an unfair advantage or attempting to profit from the misfortune of others.

Secondly, people would begin to be treated differently in the workplace. Service would improve, compassion would be allowed and even promoted, and loyalty would begin to creep back into the relationship between employer and employee. Cooperation would replace competition, or at least competition would be fair and practiced in the spirit of love.

If this sounds Pollyannaish or even impossible, it probably is. It would be like having the kingdom of God on earth "as it is in heaven." But as Jesus pointed out, "nothing is impossible with God."

In fact, the workplace is exactly where the great majority of us are *supposed* to carry out our Christian mission. But we are supposed to be like salt or light or leaven there, operating with a different agenda, on a different set of values, practicing a different spirituality from those who do not believe that God is present there.

A note of caution is needed here. We do not practice our spirituality in the workplace to show how "holier than thou" we are. Just the opposite is true in many ways. It is by how we act in the workplace—especially how we treat others—that should set us apart, *not* how pious we are or how much we talk about our religion.

Spirituality of work is about becoming aware of the divine presence in our work and allowing that presence to change how we do our work. What will be noticed by our co-workers is not our religious attitude or practice, but how we perform our work. In other words, if we're going to have a bumper sticker on our back at work that says "Honk if you love Jesus," then we'd better not cut people off in traffic!

Sharing

How has awareness of God's presence at work changed how I do (or did) my work?

- How do I react when someone talks about his or her religion or prays or performs some pious practice in the workplace?
- If there is one person in my workplace who bugs me, what is it about the person that bothers me? Do I contribute to the problem? Do I think God is inviting me to change in any way?
- How do I like to be treated at work? How does it make me feel when I am treated that way? Specifically, how will I relate to others or treat them in the way they might want to be treated?

Act

Determine a specific action (individual or group) that flows from the content of your sharing. This should be your primary consideration. When choosing an individual action, determine what you will do and share it with the group. When choosing a group action, determine who will take responsibility for different aspects of the action. The following are secondary suggestions.

Some Suggestions

- Pick one person out in your workplace, either at random or someone with whom you've been having difficulty, and spend the next week doing "random acts of kindness" to and for the person. Take note of the results, if any.

- Talk to a co-worker this week about how people treat each other in your workplace. If appropriate, discuss how you might work together to make the workplace a better place.
- Read chapters 6-7 of *Spirituality@Work*.

Look Ahead
Take time to read the "Observe" for Session 4. Be prepared to share clearly and briefly your observations at the next meeting.

Closing Prayer
Dear God, we ask for the courage to be compassionate and caring to all we encounter. Give us the desire to help others when they need help, to do unto others, as we would have them do unto us. We ask this in the name of Jesus Christ, our Lord and Savior, and in the Holy Spirit. Amen

(*Conclude with the Glory be to the Father….*)

SESSION 4

BALANCING WORK, PERSONAL, FAMILY, CHURCH, AND COMMUNITY RESPONSIBILITIES

Aim

This session tackles one of our most difficult tasks: balancing our work responsibilities with our obligations to family, church, and community. It suggests some practical steps for setting priorities and making value decisions in our lives.

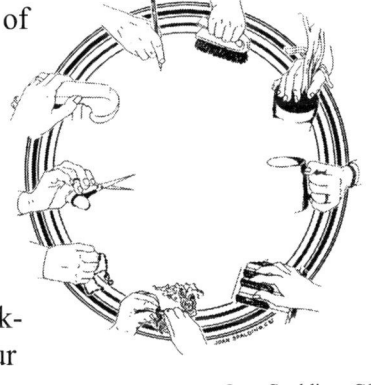

Joan Spalding, CSJ

Opening Prayer

Leader	This is the day that the Lord has made;
All	let us rejoice and be glad in it.
Leader	O let us give thanks to the Lord, for he is good,
All	for his steadfast love endures forever.

(Adapted from Psalm 118: 24, 29.)

Song: "Song over the Waters"

Scripture: Ecclesiastes 3:1-11, There is a time for everything.

Take a few moments to savor a word, a phrase, a question, or a feeling that rises up in you. Reflect on this quietly or share it aloud.

Pray together the RENEW Prayer to Mary

>Mary, you are a woman
>>wrapped in silence
>and yet the Word born of your yes
>continues to bring life to all creation.
>Mary, help us to say yes –
>to be bearers of good news
>>to a world waiting.

>Mary, you are a virgin and a mother
>empowered by the Holy Spirit.
>Help us to open ourselves
>to that same life-bringing Spirit.
>Mary, help us to say our yes.

>Mary, you are a gift of Jesus to us,
>>mother of the Church.
>Look upon our world and our lives.
>Pray for us to your Son
>>that we might be renewed
>that we might help renew
>>the face of the earth.

>Mary, help us to say yes. Amen

Action Response

Review Actions from your last meeting.

Observe
(To be prepared before the meeting.)

Talk to several people regarding the pressures and the difficulties they and their families are experiencing in finding balance in their lives. Concisely report your findings.

Judge
Reflection 1

Two of the hallmarks of the modern workplace are speed and pressure. While technology has made all our work easier in many ways, it has also made possible what was impossible a generation or even a few years ago. Computers, fax machines, the Internet, satellites, cell phones, copy machines, cable lines, overnight delivery service, cheap air travel, and the like have all made the workplace faster, but they have also created new demands. If a customer or client wants something "now," for example, it means virtually immediately.

Changing technology has also made some jobs obsolete while creating the need for ongoing training and expensive updates of both "hardware" and "software." The global economy has virtually changed the rules on how things are done and how people are to be compensated.

All of these changes have increased the demands on workers. We are now less secure in our jobs. We are asked to work longer hours, to travel more often and for longer time periods, and to relocate several times in a lifetime. Our commutes are longer and more hectic, or, on the other hand, we are asked to work out of our homes without the support systems and fringe benefits we have grown to count on.

The biggest casualty of all these changes is often our personal and family lives. Families are under increased financial pressure; relationships between spouses are stretched to the breaking point (often over work-related issues); children are left increasingly to fend for themselves and turn to television, computer games, and the Internet for diversion; divorce and child abuse are up; the education system is failing…. The list goes on and on.

Not all of this can be blamed on work, of course, but the workplace is often no help either. People are being asked to work longer hours, there is more pressure to produce, benefits are often lower, and little accommodation is made for personal and family crises or concerns.

The task of the spirituality of work is to give practitioners the value basis for making the necessary decisions needed to balance work and personal life and the courage and strength to then do so successfully. This may mean something as simple as leaving work at the same time each day; or saying no to a job assignment, transfer, or promotion; or it might mean changing jobs or careers in order to achieve a more balanced life.

Sharing
- What word, phrase, or image from the Scripture reading or the reflection touched my heart or spoke to my life?
- What are the three greatest sources of pressure on me and my family? How is each of them connected to work?
- When my work and personal/family life get out of balance, what are some of the things I do to try to get them back
in synch?

Reflection 2

Almost as difficult as balancing work with our personal and family life is this: balancing those two important aspects of life with our involvement in church and community affairs.

Changes in the Church since the Second Vatican Council have opened new areas for lay participation in church ministry. Many laypeople now serve as eucharistic ministers, lectors, catechists, and ministers of the sick. In addition, laypersons serve on parish pastoral councils, school and athletic boards, finance committees, and the like. Some become permanent deacons and share in the ministry of preaching and administering the sacraments. Others run religious education programs, youth and athletic programs, and sacramental preparation. Some laypeople become full-time or part-time "ecclesial ministers" or even pastoral associates or administrators.

These are all wonderful developments in the Church that have expanded the ministries parishes and dioceses are able to offer. They make use of the many tal-

> This is a story of a wise boss I once had. A sensitive policy problem had arisen late one Friday afternoon …but at one point my boss looked at his watch and said, "It's five minutes to Monday morning. We'll resume this discussion then."
>
> In marvelously few words, he taught me how to "let go" and to protect my family as he protected his. I have tried to live by his example ever since…. We need balance, of course. Backbone, yet flexibility. Avoiding both rigidity and flabbiness. For that we need spirit and the Spirit.
>
> Paul Provencher—social worker, husband, and father
> Norwood, Massachusetts

ents laypeople have to offer the Church. However, these lay ministries have also added to the pressures on people's lives. Many find themselves volunteering several hours per week and attending church meetings several times a month. Sometimes this takes important time away from work, personal, and family time.

Yet even as people are spending more time on church activity, they are also called to work in various community and civic organizations. This too is part of our call as Christians—to be witnesses in the world and to help transform it through our volunteer presence and political action. It is important that Catholics volunteer at local soup kitchens; walk to end hunger or racism; take leadership in neighborhood or civic organizations; campaign for issues or candidates; or even run for and hold political office themselves. Yet these activities also put additional pressure on people's lives. We sometimes feel "pulled in every direction" and "burnt out."

Only by developing a way of centering ourselves in the midst of all these conflicting obligations and responsibilities, this "frenetic activity" (as the Second Vatican Council, 1962-65, called it), can we ever hope to achieve balance in our lives.

The practice of the spirituality of our work—in all its venues and dimensions—will give us the tools to know when one sphere of life is squeezing out the others. It will give us the strength to say no to some things so that we can say yes to others and fulfill our commitments to them.

Sharing
- How many hours in an average week do I spend in

volunteer activity? Do I consider that too much, not enough, or just about right? Why?
- How do I know when my life is getting out of balance? When it does, how do I center myself?
- What is one thing in my life that I should say no to at this time? Why? What would happen if I did? What will I say no to?

Act

Determine a specific action (individual or group) that flows from the content of your sharing. This should be your primary consideration. When choosing an individual action, determine what you will do and share it with the group. When choosing a group action, determine who will take responsibility for different aspects of the action. The following are secondary suggestions.

Some Suggestions

- Sit down with yourself or with your family or loved ones and decide what is "enough" money to live comfortably, "enough" time to spend on work or volunteer activities, "enough" effort to put into various projects. Write down your conclusions and tape them to your refrigerator door. Try to stick to them.

- If you think your parish is sponsoring too much activity that is putting pressure on individuals or families, ask for a meeting with the parish staff. Explain your concerns and suggest that the parish develop some guidelines for lay activity. Offer to help with this process.

Finding God at Work

- Spend some time journaling what success means to you and record your goals. Share this journal with a friend or loved one who knows you well and ask that person to tell you how honest you are being in your reflections.
- Read chapters 9-10 of *Spirituality@Work*.

Look Ahead
Take time to read the "Observe" for Session 5. Be prepared to share clearly and briefly your observations at the next meeting.

Closing Prayer
Dear God, thank you for the gift of life, for the many freedoms and blessings you've given us. Thank you for our families and our church, work, and civic communities. Inspire us to look for the goodness in the people who are part of these communities. Help us to bring your love to each of these environments.

(Pause for prayers of petition and thanksgiving. Response: Grant us your peace, O Lord.)

SESSION 5

DECIDING RIGHT AND WRONG AT WORK

Aim

This session analyzes the difficulties in making ethical decisions at work. It uses the concept of "sins of omission" from Catholic teaching to look at "what we have failed to do" in our workplace.

Opening Prayer

Dear Jesus, thank you for teaching us how to pray and how to act toward our neighbor. Open our minds and hearts as we share with one another our thoughts and feelings. Amen

Ansgar Holmberg, CSJ

Song: "God of Day and God of Darkness"

Scripture: Micah 6:6-8, What God requires

Take a few moments to savor a word, a phrase, a question, or a feeling that rises up in you. Reflect on this quietly or share it aloud.

Pray Psalm 16 antiphonally, that is, dividing the group in two with each side alternately praying a verse.

Side 1   Protect me, O God, for in you I take refuge.

Side 2   I say to the LORD, "You are my Lord; I have no good apart from you."

Side 1   As for the holy ones in the land, they are the noble, in whom is all my delight.

Side 2   Those who choose another god multiply their sorrows; their drink offerings of blood I will not pour out or take their names upon my lips.

Side 1   The LORD is my chosen portion and my cup; you hold my lot.

Side 2   The boundary lines have fallen for me in pleasant places; I have a goodly heritage.

Side 1   I bless the LORD who gives me counsel; in the night also my heart instructs me.

Side 2   I keep the LORD always before me; because he is at my right hand, I shall not be moved.

Side 1   Therefore my heart is glad, and my soul rejoices; my body also rests secure.

Side 2   For you do not give me up to Sheol, or let your faithful one see the Pit.

All   You show me the path of life. In your presence there is fullness of joy; in your right hand are pleasures forevermore.

Action Response

Review Actions from your last meeting.

Observe
(To be prepared before the meeting.)

Ask several people what ethical issues they face or have faced in their profession, occupation, or specific workplace. Record into which of the following categories each issue fits:

The answer as to what is right or wrong is clear to the person.

The person could defend going either way on an ethical question.

The person is not at all sure what the right thing to do would be.

Report only the number of issues in each category.

Judge
Reflection 1
Most of us are not faced with major ethical issues in our workplaces on a daily basis. If we know something is wrong—and especially if it is also illegal—we simply do not do it. For most of us, in other words, if things are "black and white" we tend to do the right thing. What most of us have to worry about in the workplace are the "gray" areas, the things that are not obviously right or wrong, the decisions that are not clear, the questions that are a little ambiguous.

For example, most people struggle with how hard they are supposed to work. Should our nose always be to the grindstone? What, exactly, is "a fair day's work for a fair day's pay"? Is the customer

> I worked for a CEO ... who comes closer to living the spirituality of work than anyone I have known .... Her power came from her vision, not just from the authority she held by virtue of her position. She was gentle in her correction or direction of others—affirming but not mushy. ... She always listened before deciding anything. She was able to change her mind, but she was also deeply convinced about her own values. She treated others like she wanted to be treated, and others who worked for her eventually began to behave that way too.
>
> Timothy J. Schmaltz—social worker, teacher, writer, husband, father, and grandfather Phoenix, Arizona

really always right, and if not, how should a customer who is wrong be treated? If the goods or services we are providing people aren't harming them, is that enough? Perhaps our work is not polluting the environment, but are we contributing to the depletion of the world's resources?

How do we answer such questions? Many people merely ignore them, but those of us who practice the spirituality of work cannot. For what we seek is *integrity*, that is, we are trying to achieve a unity or wholeness that allows us to be the same person in all aspects of life—whether we are on the job, at home with our family, or involved in church or community affairs.

For example, if we believe in the equality of all people at home or in Church, then we cannot go into the workplace and discriminate against people on the basis of gender, race, or economic background. If we teach our children to be honest, we cannot lie or steal at work.

The "bottom line" on deciding to do what is right or wrong at work is never-ending, seldom obvious, and always in need of revisiting. Therefore, simple rules or solutions are almost never helpful. Instead, we, practitioners of the spirituality of work, are constantly reflecting on what we are doing and how we are doing it—with an eye toward always doing it more honestly and justly. The question we constantly ask ourselves is, What is the loving thing to do in this specific situation? not Will I get caught? or Is it required by law? And then we try to do the loving thing.

Sharing

- What word, phrase, or image from the Scripture reading or the reflection touched my heart or spoke to my life?
- What are some ethical issues I face in my place of work? How do I decide what is the right thing to do?
- Could I work for an employer who was making or selling a product (such as cigarettes) that was harmful to people? Why or why not?
- How do I decide what is "the loving thing to do"? What are the process and the criteria that I use? What "loving thing" will I do at work?

Reflection 2

When we come together at Mass or a Communion service, very early on we ask God and each other for forgiveness "for what we have done and for what we have failed to do." This idea of "sins of omission" is a very important concept in deciding to do right or wrong at work. We can never be content with "Well, I didn't do anything wrong." We also have to ask ourselves what we might have done that we did not do.

Furthermore, the more power and prestige that we have in our workplace, the more responsibility we have to do what we can to do the right thing. The Good Samaritan, for example, had the wherewithal to help the man beaten by robbers; and so he did, even though had he walked by, as did the priest and the Levite, perhaps no one would have noticed.

In many ways, we Catholics in the United States are

now part of the "establishment." Over one-third of the CEOs of Fortune 500 companies are Catholic. The largest single denomination represented in Congress is Catholic. We are in leadership positions in education, health care, the military, government, industry, unions, and so forth. We have more *power* in the workplace to do good than did previous generations of Catholics, and because we have more power we also have more *responsibility*.

This is true not just at the top levels, however. Even those of us who run small businesses, or are in middle management positions, or work for ourselves, or are retired, or raising children have an obligation to help make the workplace more like the way God would have it. This is not just a matter of avoiding things that are wrong, but it involves seeing how our workplace could be better, and then doing something to make that happen.

Sharing

- Was there ever a time that I erred on the side of *not* doing something? What happened? How did I feel?

- One positive change that needs to be made in my workplace that I have the power to implement is

  _____.

- What might happen if we Christians, in concert with people of other faith traditions, were to exercise our collective power in the workplace for the common good? What will we do?

Act

Determine a specific action (individual or group) that flows from the content of your sharing. This should be your primary consideration. When choosing an individual action, determine what you will do and share it with the group. When choosing a group action, determine who will take responsibility for different aspects of the action. The following are secondary suggestions.

Some Suggestions
- In the next month, seek to make one change in your workplace—either by stopping something that is happening that is clearly wrong or by making a change that would make things better. Pick something that you have the power to implement on your own or with the help of others in your workplace.
- Investigate a company or institution that you believe uses unjust practices. Involve others in your research and response, and determine what it would take to make significant changes.
- Talk with the homilists at your parish about the need to incorporate the idea of "sins of omission" into their preaching by using specific examples from the workplace.
- Read chapters 8 and 12 of *Spirituality@Work*.

Look Ahead

Take time to read th "Observe" for Session 6. Be prepared to share clearly and briefly your observations at the next meeting.

Closing Prayer

We ask forgiveness and mercy, Lord, for our sins of omission.

Response: Lord, have mercy.

For the times we ignored the needs of another, we pray…R

For the times we discriminated against another person or a group of people because of their gender, race, or economic background, we pray…R

For the times we were not completely honest with another, we pray…R

For the times we contributed to the depletion of earth's resources, we pray…R

For the times we failed to confront an unjust situation, we pray…R

(Please add your own intentions.) We pray…R

We ask for strength, O Lord, to do the right thing, the loving thing. We ask for the courage to deal honestly and justly with one another. Give us the desire to be disciples in the workplace so that we may have compassion for all those we encounter. Amen

SESSION 6

WORKING TO MAKE THE SYSTEM WORK

Aim

This session promotes social justice—the idea that the institutions, laws, and customs of society must work for everyone, as a basic component of the spirituality of work. Elements of Catholic social teaching such as "the common good" and "subsidiarity" are explored for their relevance and usefulness in the workplace.

Charlotte Carter Attenbery, CSJ

Opening Prayer

Lord, you said that where two or three are gathered in your name, you would be with us. We acknowledge your presence and ask you to enlighten us in order that we may learn from one another. Amen

Song: "Let Justice Roll Like a River"

Scripture: Matthew 6:25-33, Strive first for the kingdom of God.

Take a few moments to savor a word, a phrase, a question, or a feeling that rises up in you. Reflect on this quietly or share it aloud.

Action Response

Review Actions from your last meeting.

Finding God at Work

Observe
(To be prepared before the meeting.)
Ask two or three people—co-workers, family, neighbors, parishioners—if there is a policy, law, procedure, regulation, or custom in their workplace, community, or parish that is clearly not working for the common good.

Judge
Reflection 1

No matter how spiritual we are at our work as individuals, if the system itself under which we are working is flawed, we cannot do our best work.

For example, let's take a nurse in a hospital. She may find great meaning in her work, viewing it as a service to others, a vocation, a share in God's ongoing creation. She may treat her colleagues, her supervisors, the people she supervises, her patients and their families with respect and compassion. Her own life might be in perfect balance. She juggles well her responsibilities to her husband and children, her

> *When I joined my current company, it was with a quite different purpose. I had decided that what I truly enjoyed most was hands-on project work, and my new employer offered the opportunity to say "Enough!" to the demands of continually searching for advancement.*
>
> *In return, I am more at peace with myself ... and that peace has carried over into my family .... I believe that we are at our best when we know our real abilities and limitations, and being able to say "Enough already!" without regret or second guesses is a big step toward getting there.*
>
> Daniel Minarik—engineer, husband, father, and grandfather
> Buffalo Grove, Illinois

involvement in her parish, and her commitments to her community. When she sees something that is wrong—or even, could be done better—at work, she moves immediately to correct it if she can.

But if the hospital in which she works is poorly managed, if there is not enough good staff or supplies are short, or if the physical plant is inadequate, then that nurse cannot do her best, most spiritual work. If thousands of patients are coming into the hospital with inadequate insurance so that they cannot afford the care they need, or put off seeking it until they are very ill, then that nurse cannot do her best, most spiritual work. In other words, if the *system* itself does not work, then that nurse cannot do her best, most spiritual work.

This is true in virtually every kind of work, even our volunteer work, or our unpaid work around the home or with loved ones. If "the system"—the institutions of society—do not work, then none of us can do our best, most spiritual work. So part of the spirituality of work, of necessity, is working to make the system work. This is not something most of us think much about, because we assume that the system *is* working and that if it is not, somebody else will fix it.

Secondly, even if we recognize that the system needs fixing, most of us do not have the knowledge, the skill, the time, or the power to fix it. "Making the system work" seems like such a mammoth undertaking, something that is difficult and messy and controversial. It is all that, which is why we need a spirituality of work to sustain us as we attempt it.

Finding God at Work

For the act of making the system work requires organization. If individuals could make the system work by their own individual action, they would do so. To change institutions and structures of society requires leadership, political will, and sustained effort over a long period. And making changes *will* be controversial, because the system is the way it is because *somebody* is benefiting from it; and those who are benefiting from the way things are will certainly fight to keep things that way.

> *To add depth to my work, I have treated myself to taking courses to obtain a certificate in holistic nursing. The first part of this program is self-caring. I am asked to commit myself to time for the exploration of my own body-mind-spirit. .... It is the consistent rhythm of everyday practice that will help us see and live our work as a spiritual path .... I find that the deadlines of this coursework offer me the structure I need. It opens me to God's speaking to me ... about how I can help nurses and other caregivers see the spirituality of their work.*
>
> Julia Balzer Briley—nurse, author, speaker, wife, and mother
> Cumming, Georgia

So, back to our nurse at the hospital. If she really wants to do her best, most spiritual work, then she has no choice but to get involved in fixing the system—whether it is her own hospital or the health care system in general. This means that she will have to spend some of her time going to meetings, sitting on committees, talking with her fellow workers or the patients and families, perhaps joining a union or worker/management team or community organization. She might have to go to her parish and ask the members to get involved.

But only if she wants to do her best, most spiritual work. The same is true for you in your work.

Sharing
- What word, phrase, or image from the Scripture reading or the reflection touched my heart or spoke to my life?
- Have I ever been involved in an attempt to change "the system"? Describe what happened.
- When I think about getting involved in changing the system in my workplace, what concerns me the most?
- If all Catholics, or all Christians, or all people of good will worked to make the system work, what do I think the world would look like? Describe how it would "work."

Reflection 2

Catholic social teaching has several key concepts that are very helpful in "making the system work." First is the distinction between three forms of justice: commutative justice, distributive justice, and social justice.

Commutative justice is simple fairness or honesty. If I give you five dollars, you give me five dollars worth of goods or services. Commutative justice means that we don't cheat each other, take advantage of someone, or try to gain an unfair advantage. The *Catechism of the Catholic Church* teaches:

> Even if it does not contradict the provisions of civil law, any form of unjustly taking and keeping the property of others is against the seventh commandment: thus, deliberate retention of

goods lent or of objects lost; business fraud; paying unjust wages; forcing up prices by taking advantage of the ignorance or hardship of another (*CCC* 2409).

Distributive justice recognizes that not everyone has been equally blessed—with resources, with opportunity, with talent—and that love demands we try to make up for those inequalities. This is the area of charity and generosity, where those who have more give to those who have less. Distributive justice also "regulates what the community owes its citizens in proportion to their contributions and needs" (*CCC* 2411).

Social justice is about "making the system work." It says that commutative and distributive justice are not enough; that we must work to maintain or change the very structures and institutions of society so that they work for everyone. Social justice involves organization and political involvement, and often conflict and controversy.

> Society ensures social justice when it provides the conditions that allow associations or individuals to obtain what is their due, according to their nature and their vocation. Social justice is linked to the common good and the exercise of authority (*CCC* 1928).

Catholic parishes are pretty good about teaching commutative justice, and most of them are also good at encouraging distributive justice. But doing social justice is much more difficult, and it is the least understood and least talked about in most parishes.

Two other concepts from Catholic social teaching are

also important: subsidiarity and the common good.

Subsidiarity means that we should solve problems at the lowest or most local level possible. So, if we are trying to make the system work, we try to do so first in our own workplaces, families, parishes, or communities. Only when it becomes clear that the system cannot work at that level do we move to higher levels of society or church.

The *common good* is the idea that we do not look out only for our narrow self-interest, either as individuals or even as Catholics. We are called to respect all persons and the natural world, to work to bring about the social well-being and development of peoples, to work for peace and justice for *everyone*, not just ourselves. And so we are asked to make the system work for everyone, including ourselves. (See *CCC* 1905-1912.)

All of these concepts from Catholic social teaching are useful in our attempts to make the system work.

Sharing

- Some examples from my own work of commutative, distributive, and social justice are _____.

- What is the relationship between the common good and self-interest? Are the two mutually exclusive? Why or why not?
- When did I make a decision that was beneficial both for the common good and for myself?
- How would subsidiarity function in my own workplace, family, parish, diocese, or in the universal Church?

- How might I use the idea of subsidiarity to solve a current problem in my family or workplace? How will I do it?

Act

Determine a specific action (individual or group) that flows from the content of your sharing. This should be your primary consideration. When choosing an individual action, determine what you will do and share it with the group. When choosing a group action, determine who will take responsibility for different aspects of the action. The following are secondary suggestions.

Some Suggestions

- Take a specific societal system—health care, criminal justice, education, for example—and research whether the system is working. Talk to someone you know who works in that system or is served by it. Go to a public hearing or meeting on the issue. (Walk through one of the institutions in the system.) Observe first-hand what is going on. As you do these things, pray and listen to the Spirit of God in your heart. Join or organize a group to deal with the issue you have researched, either at your workplace or in your parish or community.

- Talk to someone in your workplace about social justice matters at least once a month, perhaps over lunch or on a break or while going back or forth to work. See if together you can come up with a way to act in concert on one matter discussed.

- Read more about the various kinds of justice in the *Catechism of the Catholic Church*, particularly,

Article 7, The Seventh Commandment, 2401-2463, and Article 3, Social Justice, 1928-1938.

- Read chapter 11 of *Spirituality@Work*.

Closing Prayer

Dear Lord, there is in this world so much to do. Help us to cooperate with you in bringing about peace and justice, joy and love. Help us to grow in faith, hope, and charity so we may be even closer to you and your people.

(*Share prayers of thanksgiving*. Response: Thank you, O Lord.)

Music Resources
GIA Publications, Inc.
7404 South Mason Avenue
Chicago, IL 60638

Phone   800-442-1358 or 708-496-3800
Fax   708-496-3828
Web site   www.giamusic.com
E-mail   custserv@giamusic.com

Further Reading on the Spirituality of Work

The Active Life: A Spirituality of Work, Creativity, and Caring by Parker Palmer (San Francisco: Harper & Row, 1988)

Crossing the Unknown Sea: Work as a Pilgrimage of Identity by David Whyte (New York: Riverhead Books, 2001)

Full-time Christians: The Real Challenge of Vatican II by William Droel (Mystic, Connecticut: Twenty-Third Publications, 2002)

Jesus and His Message: An Introduction to the Good News by Rev. Leo Mahon (Chicago: ACTA Publications, 2000)

The Practice of the Presence of God by Brother Lawrence, updated in today's language by Ellyn Sanna, (Urichville, Ohio: Barbour Publishing, Inc., 1998)

Titles in IMPACT Series

Sacramental Pathways
- Preparing for Your Child's Baptism
- In Memory of Jesus: Reflections for Parents Whose Children Are Preparing for First Eucharist
- At Home in the Catholic Church

Faith in Daily Life
- Finding God@Work: Practicing Spirituality in Your Workplace
- The Wisdom Years: Discovering Meaning and Purpose
- Grieving the Death of a Loved One
- Make Media Work for You
- Making God Visible: Parenting Young Children
- Nurturing Our Commitment: The Early Married Years
- Strengthening Family Life
- The World of Work

Spiritual Awakenings
- At Prayer with Mary
- Awakening the Mystic Within: Graced Vision
- Lenten Longings: Let Yourself Be…, Cycle A
- Lenten Longings: For the Life of the World, Cycle B
- Lenten Longings: Seeing with God's Eyes, Cycle C

Finding God at Work

Discipleship in Action
- Beginnings: Human and World Issues
- Reflections on "Dead Man Walking" (capital punishment)
- Embracing Life
- Beyond Black & White
- Civic Responsibility: What's It All About?
- Discipleship of Nonviolence
- Hunger in God's World

About RENEW International

RENEW International continues its work of parish spiritual renewal and evangelization, creating the climate for God's transforming grace in and among individuals and communities, neighborhoods, and the world.

RENEW International services include the following areas:

RENEW: Spiritual Renewal for the 21st Century
This 3-year parish spiritual renewal and evangelization process implements the U.S. Bishops' documents, *Go and Make Disciples* and *Our Hearts Were Burning Within Us*. SCC materials are available in 12 languages and 4 customized options. All trainings and leadership materials are provided in English and Spanish.

Why Catholic? Journey through the Catechism
Why Catholic? offers a concrete approach to help adults form their Catholic faith and connect its teachings to their everyday lives. With its thorough exploration of the *Catechism of the Catholic Church*, this process encourages learning in a prayerful small-community setting. The faith-sharing materials offer 48 sessions on Catholic beliefs, sacraments, morality, and prayer, with direct *Catechism* quotes, scriptural references, and reflection questions. Includes a full range of elements in English and Spanish: orientation, small community leader formation, retreat experiences, invitation video, bulletin inserts, etc., which enable parishes and dioceses to gain the full benefit of this meaningful process. For more information on this new and excellent program, go to www.whycatholic.org.

Healing the Body of Christ

The specially designed program, based on the RENEW parish process, fosters healing and spiritual renewal in the wake of the abuse crisis in the Church. Themes center on the Church's teachings on the Body of Christ—how its members' actions impact this Body and how the Body can be healed and brought to greater holiness by God through the gifts of Scripture, Eucharist, and the other sacraments. Training and small group materials are available in both English and Spanish.

RENEW Resources

Over 50 titles are designed for SCCs, seasonal small groups, ministries, parish leadership and enrichment. Innovative and in-depth offerings include books, videos, faith-sharing reflections for parish committees and councils, topical and seasonal faith-sharing books for small communities, pamphlets, and prayer cards. Many are available in Spanish and English.

ParishLife.com

This subscription-based Web site hosts an extensive selection of in-depth topics on Catholic life and teaching, downloadable workshops, and days of reflection, bulletin boards, and chat rooms. *Great Ideas from Great Parishes* provides access to the best practices and pastoral ideas from parishes worldwide.

RENEW Worldwide

Parishes outside of North America are led through a 3-year spiritual renewal process similar to RENEW. The Worldwide Team works in countries including England, El Salvador, Honduras, India, Ireland, Lithuania, New Zealand, Nigeria, Northern Ireland, Rwanda, Slovakia, and Uganda.

> Download free sample sessions of various titles at our online bookstore at www.renewintl.org.
> Order online or toll free 888-433-3221.
> Join our Online Community at www.renewintl.org.